Instant Nagios Starter

An easy guide to getting a Nagios server up and
running for monitoring, altering, and reporting

Michael Guthrie

BIRMINGHAM - MUMBAI

Instant Nagios Starter

First published: May 2013

Production Reference: 1170513

Published by Packt Publishing Ltd.
Livery Place
35 Livery Street
Birmingham B3 2PB, UK.

ISBN 978-1-78216-250-6

www.packtpub.com

Credits

Author

Michael Guthrie

Reviewer

Manish Kumar

Acquisition Editor

Edward Gordon

Commissioning Editor

Sruthi Kutty

Technical Editor

Veena Pagare

Project Coordinator

Sherin Padayatty

Proofreader

Lydia Morris

Graphics

Ronak Dhruv

Production Coordinators

Aditi Gajjar

Prachali Bhiwandkar

Cover Work

Aditi Gajjar

Cover Image

Sheetal Aute

About the Author

Michael Guthrie is the lead developer at Nagios enterprises and has developed new features and add-ons for Nagios Core, Nagios XI, and Nagios Fusion. Michael started his IT career at Nagios Enterprises as a student developer writing documentation and new components for Nagios Core and Nagios XI, as well as giving technical support. At work, Michael particularly enjoys working on UI development, performance tuning, and data visualizations. When he's not at work he enjoys spending time with his family, being outside, and working on his house.

Michael started his jobs at Nagios Enterprises by writing a substantial amount of documentation for Nagios XI, which is now the Nagios XI Administrator's Manual.

First, I would like to thank Ethan Galstad for creating Nagios, and giving me the opportunity at Nagios Enterprises to work with this great project. I would like to thank Mike Weber from Spidertools, for the outstanding Nagios training I received when I first started working there. I'd like to thank all of the community developers who contribute to Nagios and its surrounding projects. I'd also like to thank my fellow techs here, at Nagios Enterprises for helping to proofread my work and test out my instructions. I'm thankful to my family for giving me the reason to bring my best to work every day, and to the Lord for leading me to the most rewarding job I've ever had.

About the Reviewer

Manish Kumar (manikumar85@gmail.com) is a Nagios Certified Professional, and has more than five years of experience in monitoring and management of enterprise systems and networks. Previously being involved in the development of enterprise grade network monitoring and management solution "EDGE" while working at C-DAC, Manish continues to enjoy working on development, implementation, integration, and customization of open source tools, and is keen on providing open source solutions to the infrastructure management services business need. He is a FOSS enthusiast, contributor, and passionate about working on open source tools and technologies. Years back he almost had a crush on Unix, and still loves and enjoys working on it, his recent crush being open source cloud computing platforms.

I am thankful to my close friends and my family for being extremely supportive throughout the duration, and for their constant encouragement and patience to let me take my time out for the work.

www.packtpub.com

Support files, eBooks, discount offers and more

You might want to visit www.packtpub.com for support files and downloads related to your book.

Did you know that Packt offers eBook versions of every book published, with PDF and ePub files available? You can upgrade to the eBook version at www.packtpub.com and as a print book customer, you are entitled to a discount on the eBook copy. Get in touch with us at service@ packtpub.com for more details.

At www.packtpub.com, you can also read a collection of free technical articles, sign up for a range of free newsletters and receive exclusive discounts and offers on Packt books and eBooks.

packtlib.packtpub.com

Do you need instant solutions to your IT questions? PacktLib is Packt's online digital book library. Here, you can access, read and search across Packt's entire library of books.

Why Subscribe?

- ✦ Fully searchable across every book published by Packt
- ✦ Copy and paste, print and bookmark content
- ✦ On demand and accessible via web browser

Free Access for Packt account holders

If you have an account with Packt at www.packtpub.com, you can use this to access PacktLib today and view nine entirely free books. Simply use your login credentials for immediate access.

Table of Contents

Instant Nagios Starter

Welcome to *Instant Nagios Starter*. This book has been created to provide you with all the information that you need to get Nagios installed and monitoring your environment. You will learn the fundamentals of how Nagios works, and how to utilize it to monitor just about anything in your infrastructure, whether it's a small office or a large organization. This document contains the following sections:

So what is Nagios explains what Nagios actually is, how it works, and how you can use it to monitor virtually anything.

Installation helps you learn how to download and quickly install Nagios with the minimum fuss, and then set it up so that you can use it as soon as possible.

Quick Start will show you how to begin monitoring hosts and services using several of the different methods available for monitoring with Nagios.

Top 5 features you need to know about will examine some of the primary features that every Nagios user should understand. This section will cover Nagios checks, configuration management, incident management, and reporting.

People and places you should get to know helps you learn how to get additional resources to extend the capabilities of Nagios, how to resolve problems, and where to get help. Nagios has limitless flexibility and an enormous community of projects surrounding it.

So, what is Nagios?

Nagios is an infrastructure monitoring solution utilized to monitor just about any aspect of network infrastructure or application health. The heart of Nagios revolves around two primary concepts—scheduling checks and responding to events. Nagios takes in a user-defined configuration of hosts, services, and contacts, and schedules checks to be run at regular intervals to verify the health of various hosts and services. When the status of a host or service changes, Nagios triggers an event, and can take actions such as sending an e-mail or opening a ticket in an external ticketing application. What's so great about Nagios as a technology? In a simple word—flexibility—as shown in the following bullet list:

✦ Nagios does all of its monitoring through the user-defined check plugins, which are various scripts and binaries developed to monitor a specific metric or status. This means that there is no limit to what can be monitored by Nagios. If anything plugs into or runs on a computer, it can be monitored by Nagios.

✦ Thousands of check plugins have been developed by the Nagios community to monitor virtually any type of hardware or software.

✦ Nagios continually schedules and initiates regular checks of monitored hosts and services. Any host or service check that Nagios schedules and executes is known as an **active check**.

✦ Nagios responds to host or service state changes, or events, using user-definable event handlers, which can be anything from a simple mail command to a custom script that automatically fixes the problem that was detected.

✦ Nagios can also act as a listener to simply receive and process check results from remote locations. These are known as **passive checks**.

✦ Nagios can be extended with various add-ons to provide data visualization, historical trending, and large environment scalability.

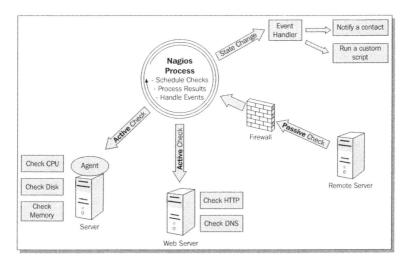

Installation

Nagios can be installed in multiple ways. Many users prefer package installations, but this tutorial will cover a source installation of Nagios Core because of its platform independence and consistency with the Nagios Core documentation. Nagios requires knowledge of certain key files and directories, so having these locations match the Core documentation should simplify the learning process. The instructions for these section are tested and verified for RHEL/CentOS based Linux distributions, and all commands in the following sections should be run as the root user.

In five easy steps, you can install Nagios, and get it set up on your system. If you wish to skip manual installation altogether, you can also download a pre-installed virtual machine from `http://www.nagios.org/download`, which includes Nagios Core, Nagios plugins, PNP performance graphing, and several other key add-ons.

Step 1 – What do I need?

Before you install Nagios, you will need to check that you have all of the required elements, listed as follows:

+ A freshly installed Linux platform, I recommend CentOS. Nagios should generally be installed on a dedicated server, either a physical machine or virtual machine.

+ Memory: 256 MB (min), 1 GB (recommended).

+ Nagios requires the `wget httpd php gcc glibc glibc-common gd gd-devel make net-snmp` packages (or their platform equivalents).

+ Hardware based on environment size. There's no easy formula to determine hardware specs for larger Nagios environments, but the general rule is—*the larger the environment, the faster the disks, and the more CPU cores you'll need*. Plan on a minimum of one CPU core per 500 hosts being monitored.

Step 2 – Prerequisites

The following code example will describe how to install prerequisite packages for both CentOS/RHEL-based distributions, and create users that are necessary for Nagios to run.

Run the following command from a command-line shell to install required packages for source installation:

```
yum install -y autoconf wget httpd php gcc glibc glibc-common gd gd-devel
make net-snmp xinetd openssl-devel unzip
```

Now let's set up user permissions for the Nagios process using the following commands:

```
useradd nagios
groupadd nagcmd
usermod -a -G nagcmd nagios
```

Downloading the example code

You can download the example code files for all Packt books you have purchased from your account at `http://www.packtpub.com`. If you purchased this book elsewhere, you can visit `http://www.packtpub.com/support` and register to have the files e-mailed directly to you.

Step 3 – Downloading and extracting Nagios and Nagios plugins

The easiest way to download Nagios is as a compressed tarball from `http://www.nagios.org/download`.

The following example demonstrates downloading the latest packages at the time of writing this book. We suggest that you download the most current stable build of both the Nagios Core and Nagios plugins tarballs. Lets get both of these packages downloaded and extracted into the `/tmp` directory:

```
cd /tmp
wget http://prdownloads.sourceforge.net/sourceforge/nagios/nagios-
3.5.0.tar.gz
wget http://prdownloads.sourceforge.net/sourceforge/nagiosplug/nagios-
plugins-1.4.16.tar.gz
tar zxf nagios-3.5.0.tar.gz
tar zxf nagios-plugins-1.4.16.tar.gz
```

Step 4 – Compiling and installing

A typical Nagios installation is made up of more than just the Nagios Core monitoring engine. The list of available add-ons for Nagios is quite large, but the following steps will guide you through the installation and setup of the key packages required for almost all Nagios installations. The following steps will guide you through installing Nagios Core, Nagios plugins, NRPE for remote agent monitoring, and NRDP for passive monitoring.

Nagios Core

The following commands will demonstrate how to compile Nagios Core and Nagios plugins from the source tarballs downloaded from the previous step, and how to install all the necessary files for Nagios Core to run and begin monitoring:

```
cd /tmp/nagios
./configure --with-command-group=nagcmd
make all
```

```
make install
make install-init
make install-config
make install-commandmode
make install-webconf
```

Nagios plugins

As mentioned earlier, Nagios monitors hosts and services through the execution of check commands, so let's go ahead and install the Nagios plugins bundle as well using the commands:

```
cd /tmp/nagios-plugins-1.4.16
./configure
make
make install
```

The following commands will verify the Nagios object configuration and start the monitoring engine:

```
/usr/local/nagios/bin/nagios -v /usr/local/nagios/etc/nagios.cfg
/etc/init.d/nagios start
```

From here, the monitoring engine should be up and running.

Step 5 – The Nagios directory structure

The locations for Nagios files will vary depending on whether or not you've installed from source or a packaged version, and most Nagios add-ons require knowledge of where many of these key files are located. The following list outlines some key files and locations in your Nagios installation for a source installation:

+ `/usr/local/nagios/etc`: This directory contains all configuration files related to the monitoring configuration.

+ `/usr/local/nagios/var`: This directory contains Nagios logs and all runtime data files such as `status.dat`, `nagios.lock`, and `objects.cache`. These files are commonly used by various Nagios add-ons as a data source.

+ `/usr/local/nagios/libexec`: This directory contains all of the Nagios plugins that can be run for the various host or service checks.

+ `/usr/local/nagios/bin`: This directory contains all of the binary executable files used by Nagios and often by key add-ons that may get installed.

+ `/usr/local/Nagios/sbin`: This directory contains all compiled web CGI's used by the web interface.

+ `/usr/local/Nagios/share`: This directory contains all web-accessible files such has PHP, HTML, CSS, and image files.

Step 6 – Installing NRPE and NRDP

The preceding steps are required for all the Nagios installations to function at any level. However, most environments will require monitoring data for information that cannot be accessed externally on a host machine. For example, CPU load or memory usage are sets of data that can't be accessed on a remote machine without some sort of agent or internal script that has access to that data. Some users utilize SNMP or WMI to access this data for Nagios, but both of these methods require more advanced setup methods, and don't scale as well as the two methods described in the following sections. The latest versions for both of these add-ons can be obtained from `http://exchange.nagios.org`.

NRPE

NRPE allows you to remotely execute Nagios plugins as **active checks** on remote machines by means of an **agent**. NRPE can communicate with agents on both Windows and Linux/Unix machines. NRPE contacts the agent on the remote machine, asks it to run a check command, and returns the results back to Nagios, as illustrated in the following diagram:

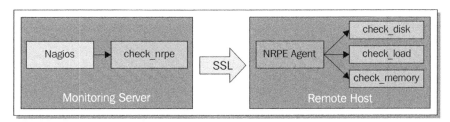

1. The following commands will install the NRPE listener on the system and add it as a sub-service of the `xinetd` daemon:

```
cd /tmp

wget http://prdownloads.sourceforge.net/sourceforge/nagios/nrpe-
2.13.tar.gz

tar zxf nrpe-2.13.tar.gz

cd nrpe-2.13

./configure --enable-command-args

make all

make install-plugin

make install-daemon

make install-xinetd

make install-daemon-config

/etc/init.d/xinetd restart
```

2. The following commands make sure that the `xinetd` service will be running each time we reboot:

```
chkconfig --add xinetd
chkconfig --level 35 xinetd on
```

3. The two key configuration files related to NRPE are `/etc/xinetd.d/nrpe` and `/usr/local/nagios/etc/nrpe.cfg`. Be sure to review these settings to make sure they are suitable for your environment.

Getting started with NRPE and active checks will be covered in the *Top features you need to know about* section.

NRPE NAGIOS REMOTE DATA PROCESSOR

NRDP functions as a form of web API to submit both check results and commands using POST and GET over standard HTTP and HTTPS ports. Using NRDP, Nagios acts as a listener for results for a host or service, while cron or some other processes run the check on their own schedule. This is known as a passive check. NRDP allows for batch submissions of passive checks, and uses an XML format for data transport. NRDP is considered to be the most lightweight way to submit passive checks to Nagios.

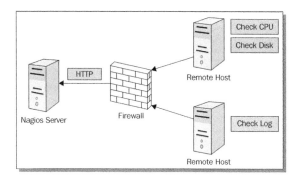

The following steps will guide you through the installation process for NRDP:

1. To install NRDP, download the latest version from Nagios and extract the files using the following commands:

```
cd /tmp
wget http://assets.nagios.com/downloads/nrdp/nrdp.zip
unzip nrdp.zip
 Copy files to the installation directory with new permissions.
mkdir /usr/local/nrdp
cd nrdp
cp -r * /usr/local/nrdp
chown -R nagios.nagios /usr/local/nrdp
```

2. Set up web access to NRDP by adding the apache alias.

 Note that on Ubuntu/Debian machines, the apache configuration directory is /etc/apache2/conf.d, while RHEL based systems store configuration files in /etc/httpd/conf.d.

```
cp nrdp.conf /etc/httpd/conf.d
/etc/init.d/httpd restart
```

3. Add at least one authorization token for remote senders to submit results or commands. Open the /usr/local/nrdp/server/config.inc.php file in a text editor and add a new token to the authorized_tokens array.

4. The following example shows two tokens added to the authorization array:

```
// NOTE: tokens are just alphanumeric strings - make them hard to
guess!
$cfg['authorized_tokens'] = array(
"asd7fjk3134",
"df23m7jadI34",
);
```

5. Save the config.inc.php file and close it. From here you can test the NRDP API, by accessing it from the following address:

```
http://<your_nagios_server_address>/nrdp
```

Submit Nagios Command:
Token:
Command: DISABLE_HOST_NOTIFICATIONS;somehost
[Submit Command]

Submit Check Data
Token:
Check Data:
```
<?xml version='1.0'?>
<checkresults>
        <checkresult type='host'>
                <hostname>somehost</hostname>
                <state>0</state>
                <output>Everything looks okay!|perfdata</output>
        </checkresult>
        <checkresult type='service'>
                <hostname>somehost</hostname>
                <servicename>someservice</servicename>
                <state>1</state>
                <output>WARNING: Danger Will Robinson!|perfdata</output>
        </checkresult>
</checkresults>
```

[Submit Check Data]

Step 7 – Post installation setup

There are a few remaining steps that should be completed after Nagios is installed to make sure everything is accessible after installation.

Web access

The following commands will verify that the apache web server is running, and will create a default account for accessing the Nagios web interface. The htpasswd command will prompt for an initial password for the nagiosadmin user.

```
/etc/init.d/httpd start
htpasswd -c /usr/local/nagios/etc/htpasswd.users nagiosadmin
```

Adding services to system startup

For RHEL/CentOS systems, the Nagios and httpd processes should be added to the chkconfig list so that they're started automatically each time the system boots. This can be accomplished by the following commands:

```
chkconfig --add nagios
chkconfig --level 35 nagios on
chkconfig --add httpd
chkconfig --level 35 httpd on
```

> Firewall and security rules are an important consideration for a monitoring server. Typically, most Linux distributions ship with both iptables and SELinux projects. Security is an important consideration with Nagios because it essentially has access keys to the entire infrastructure. For now, the following steps will disable SELinux, and open specific firewall ports to allow access for the Nagios web interface, as well as the standard ports that Nagios uses for external communication with other systems.

SELinux

SELinux functions as a secondary layer of system security in addition to firewall rules and user account privileges. However, if you are unfamiliar with black box of SELinux, it just tends to make a lot of system events fail with little to no trail on what prevented it from working, and acts more like an unnecessary middle manager. For simplicity's sake, we'll be disabling SELinux to prevent complications. Disable SELinux by updating /etc/selinux/config to match the following settings:

```
SELINUX=disabled
SETLOCALDEFS=0
```

Then run the following command to immediately disable SELinux:

```
setenforce 0
```

Firewall rules

Firewall settings are ultimately up to the administrator with regards to which ports should be allowed, but the following settings are some basic guidelines as to which ports need to be opened, and their corresponding services. On a CentOS/RHEL-based system, the following lines can be added to the /etc/sysconfig/iptables file somewhere before the COMMIT statement:

```
# HTTP/HTTPS
-A INPUT -m state --state NEW -m tcp -p tcp --dport 80 -j ACCEPT
-A INPUT -m state --state NEW -m tcp -p tcp --dport 443 -j ACCEPT
# NRPE
-A INPUT -m state --state NEW -m tcp -p tcp --dport 5666 -j ACCEPT
# NSCA
-A INPUT -m state --state NEW -m tcp -p tcp --dport 5667 -j ACCEPT
```

Once the firewall rules are in place, the iptables service will need to be restarted to apply the settings using the following command:

```
/etc/init.d/iptables restart
```

And that's it!

By this point, you should have a working installation of Nagios and you are now free to explore and discover more about it. You can access the Nagios Core interface by entering the following URL in your web browser. Replace the IP address with the IP address or host name of the machine that Nagios is installed on.

```
http://<your_nagios_server_address>/nagios
```

Enter `nagiosadmin` as the username, and the initial password created upon installation to log into the interface.

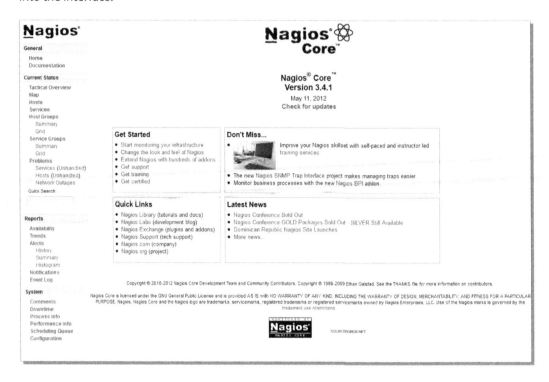

Quick start – Monitoring hosts and services

The logic of Nagios as a monitoring engine is determined by a set of **object configuration** files, which are located under the `etc` directory of the Nagios tree. For a source installation, this directory is located at `/usr/local/nagios/etc`. From the configuration files in this directory, Nagios knows what to monitor, when to monitor, who to notify, and how to respond to events. Interaction with these files is required in order to set up monitoring with Nagios, so understanding how to work with them is essential. This section will be an introduction to the basics of adding new hosts, services, contacts, and templates. A complete reference for all the Nagios configuration files is available in the Nagios core manual on `sourceforge.net`, and it is by far the best reference for a complete understanding of Nagios configuration files. It can be found at the following link:

```
http://nagios.sourceforge.net/docs/3_0/
```

Step 1 – Modifying nagios.cfg

Nagios knows which configuration files to parse by maintaining a master reference in the `nagios.cfg` file. For any new configuration file to be recognized by Nagios, either the file or the directory it is in has to be defined in `nagios.cfg`. For source installations, this file is located at `/usr/local/nagios/etc/nagios.cfg`. Perform the following steps to modify `nagios.cfg`:

1. Start by creating two new directories to store our configuration files:

   ```
   cd /usr/local/nagios/etc/objects
   mkdir hosts
   mkdir services
   ```

2. Then open `nagios.cfg` with your preferred text editor to add the new directories:

   ```
   # You can specify individual object config files as shown below:
   cfg_file=/usr/local/nagios/etc/objects/commands.cfg
   cfg_file=/usr/local/nagios/etc/objects/contacts.cfg
   cfg_file=/usr/local/nagios/etc/objects/timeperiods.cfg
   cfg_file=/usr/local/nagios/etc/objects/templates.cfg
   # Definitions for monitoring the local (Linux) host
   cfg_file=/usr/local/nagios/etc/objects/localhost.cfg
   ```

3. Add the following lines to allow all files in our `hosts` and `services` directories to be automatically added to the monitoring configuration:

   ```
   cfg_dir=/usr/local/nagios/etc/objects/hosts
   cfg_dir=/usr/local/nagios/etc/objects/services
   ```

4. Save the file and close it, it's time to add our first new host!

Step 2 – Adding a host

A **host** in Nagios is any machine or device with an IP address or a host name. The following example will demonstrate the creation of a basic host configuration file that we can add to the monitoring configuration:

1. Create a new file at /usr/local/nagios/etc/objects/hosts called test.cfg, and open it in a text editor:

    ```
    define host{
            host_name        test
            alias            test
            address          127.0.0.1
               use           linux-server
    }
    ```

2. There are many more configuration directives that can be specified for a host, but as a best practice, it's best to specify as many of these values in a template as possible.

3. Save the file and close it. You just added your first new host!

Step 3 – Adding a service

Services in Nagios are processes, applications, metrics, and anything else that can be monitored under the scope of the associated host. The following example creates a basic service definition for the test used, and will be used to start monitoring with a simple HTTP check:

1. Service configurations are created in much the same way that hosts are. Create a new file named test.cfg, at /usr/local/nagios/etc/objects/services, and open it in a text editor:

    ```
    define service{
            host_name                test
            service_description            HTTP
            check_command          check_http
               use              generic-service
    }
    ```

2. Services can be applied to a single host, a list of hosts, or even an entire host group, and check_command specified for each of them can be customized to take custom arguments as well. However, for the moment, let's start things simple and keep moving forward.

3. Save the file and close it.

Step 4 – Creating and assigning contacts

Alerting is an essential part of monitoring infrastructure with Nagios, but it is recommended to minimize or even disable the use of alerts while setting up your monitoring environment. Users who receive too many false alerts will be trained to ignore them. Setting up effective alerting starts with creating appropriate contacts and contact groups for the hosts and services that are being monitored. Contacts also form the basis for host and service permissions in Nagios. A regular-level user in Nagios will only be able to view and submit commands for hosts and services that they are contacts for, unless he/she is granted some level of global access in the `cgi.cfg` file. The following are the steps to create and assign contacts:

1. Open `/usr/local/nagios/etc/objects/contacts.cfg` in your preferred text editor.

2. By default, the `nagiosadmin` contact is already created for you. This account should typically be reserved for the top-level Nagios administrator. For other users, new contacts should be created.

3. Add a new contact definition with your preferred username and e-mail address.

    ```
    define contact{
            contact_name                    test
            use                             generic-contact
            alias                           Test User
            email                           test@example.com
            }
    ```

4. Let's also add this contact to the `admins` contact group, which already exists in the same file:

    ```
    define contactgroup{
            contactgroup_name       admins
            alias                   Nagios Administrators
            members                 nagiosadmin,test
            }
    ```

5. Save the file and close it.

6. In order to allow the access of the web interface to the new contacts, they need to be added to the `htpasswd.users` file using the following command:

    ```
    htpasswd -c /usr/local/nagios/etc/htpasswd.users test
    ```

Step 5 – Verifying configuration and restarting Nagios

All monitoring and event handling is done based on rules defined in the object configuration files, so the monitoring process requires a valid configuration in order to run. Always verify any configuration changes before attempting to restart Nagios, using the following steps. Attempting to restart Nagios with configuration errors will halt all the monitoring on the system.

1. Nagios configurations can be verified on any installation, by running the Nagios binary file with the -v flag, followed by the main nagios.cfg file. On a source installation, this command can be run as follows:

   ```
   /usr/local/nagios/bin/nagios -v /usr/local/nagios/etc/nagios.cfg
   ```

2. If all goes well, you'll see the following message verifying that there are no configuration errors and that Nagios is ready to be restarted:

   ```
   Total Warnings· 0
   Total Errors:   0
   ```

3. Things look okay. No serious problems were detected during the pre-flight check.

4. Once configuration verification succeeds, Nagios can be restarted with the following command:

   ```
   /etc/init.d/nagios restart
   ```

5. Access the web interface to see the new host and service in Nagios!

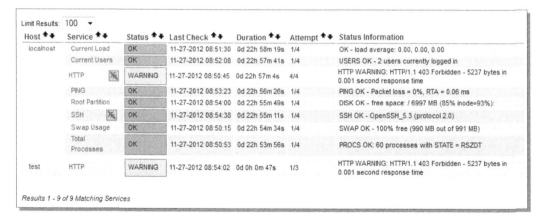

Top 5 features you'll want to know about

Nagios is an incredibly flexible monitoring solution that requires effective management and setup. So far we've covered some basic steps in getting Nagios up and running. The next steps will be to dive in and learn the primary methods used that make Nagios such an effective monitoring tool. As you review the features in this section, consider what specifically needs to be monitored, who should be accountable when problems occur, and what scenarios will best meet the needs of your environment.

Active checks using agents

Any check that Nagios schedules and executes itself is known as an **active check**. In the previous section, we covered how to perform a basic check for the HTTP service running on a particular machine. But what happens when we need to monitor something internal, such as CPU load or a process status on another machine? This information is not available for an outside machine to simply request, unless there is some sort of agent established on the remote machine that can retrieve that information.

> Monitoring agents are used to securely communicate internal system metric information to other machines that request the information. This can be any kind of data such as CPU Usage, running processes, or log data. Some users prefer to utilize existing services such as SNMP or WMI to retrieve this information for Nagios, but those methods can require more advanced setup steps and knowledge of those protocols. Two commonly used agents with Nagios are NRPE for Linux machines, and **NSClient++** for Windows machines.

Active checks with NRPE

Installing the NRPE agent on a Linux/Unix platform varies by distribution, but typically it can be installed from the platform's package manager. Nagios Enterprises has also released several quick installers for the agents that work with both Nagios Core and Nagios XI, which is the commercial version of Nagios. These quick installers handle any package prerequisites, firewall rules, and user setup for the agent to work correctly.

RHEL/CentOS

The document at the following link describes how to install the NRPE agent on RHEL and CentOS based installations:

```
http://assets.nagios.com/downloads/nagiosxi/docs/Installing_The_XI_Linux_
Agent.pdf
```

The document at the following link describes how to install the NRPE agent on Ubuntu/ Debian installations:

```
http://assets.nagios.com/downloads/nagiosxi/docs/Installing_the_Ubuntu_and_
Debian_Agent.pdf
```

The document at the following link describes how to install the NRPE agent on Solaris installations:

```
http://assets.nagios.com/downloads/nagiosxi/agents/Installing_The_XI_Solaris_
Agent.pdf
```

Nagios uses the `check_nrpe` plugin to run remote checks on client machines. Once the agent installation is completed on the client, connectivity between the Nagios server and the client machines can be verified by running the following commands, which should return the NRPE version of the client if connectivity was successful:

```
cd /usr/local/nagios/libexec
./check_nrpe -H 192.168.5.59
NRPE v2.12
```

Troubleshooting NRPE connection problems

Common problems related to NRPE connections are as follows:

- ✦ Port 5666 is closed on either the client or server machine's firewall
- ✦ SELinux restrictions may be enabled

To troubleshoot these problems, perform the following tasks:

- ✦ Verify that the Nagios server is added to the client machine's `allowed_hosts` list
- ✦ Verify that `openssl` and `openssl-devel` packages are installed and are up-to-date

Now let's take a look at fetching some internal information from this machine. The NRPE agent requires that the commands be defined on the client machines in order to prevent arbitrary commands from being sent from the Nagios server. The following are some example commands defined on my client host:

```
command[check_users]=/usr/local/nagios/libexec/check_users -w 5 -c 10
command[check_load]=/usr/local/nagios/libexec/check_load -w 15,10,5 -c
30,25,20
```

The format for defining a client command is as follows:

```
command[<name_of_command>]=/path/to/plugin <arguments>
```

So, with the commands defined previously, the following command can be run to fetch user information on the client machine from the Nagios server:

```
./check_nrpe -H 192.168.5.59 -c check_users
USERS OK - 1 users currently logged in |users=1;5;10;0
```

Using the previous command as an example, we can now create a new command definition to use it for multiple services across many hosts. Since we don't want to create a separate command for every single check_something that we want to run on an agent, we'll go ahead and create a generic check command on the Nagios server. Nagios commands typically utilize **macros**, which are essentially configuration variables that get translated at runtime. $USER1$ refers to directory location of the Nagios plugins, $HOSTADDRESS$ is the IP address or host name of the corresponding host, and $ARG1$ is the command that we're calling on the client machine. The following can be added to the /usr/local/nagios/etc/objects/commands.cfg file:

```
define command {
        command_name    check_nrpe_generic
        command_line    $USER1$/check_nrpe -H $HOSTADDRESS$ -c $ARG1$
}
```

Let's go ahead and create a new host definition in our host's directory, and some corresponding services to be monitored on that NRPE client host:

```
define host{
        host_name       My_NRPE_Host
        alias           NRPE Test Host
        address         192.168.5.59
        use             linux-server
}
define service{
        use                 generic-service
        host_name               My_NRPE_Host
        service_description   Users
        check_command           check_nrpe_generic!check_users
        }
define service{
        use                 generic-service
        host_name               My_NRPE_Host
        service_description   CPU Load
        check_command           check_nrpe_generic!check_load
        }
```

NRPE agent checks can be made to be even more flexible by allowing command arguments on the client side using the following command, which allows you to adjust arguments later on without having to make any modifications to the client machine:

```
command[check_users]=/usr/local/nagios/libexec/check_users $ARG1$
```

The Nagios server's definitions would now look like the following:

```
define command {
    command_name    check_nrpe_generic
    command_line    $USER1$/check_nrpe -H $HOSTADDRESS$ -c $ARG1$ -a
    '$ARGS2$'
}
define service{
    use             generic-service
    host_name               My_NRPE_Host
    service_description   Users
    check_command           check_nrpe_generic!check_users!'-w 5 -c 10'
}
```

This second example allows for thresholds and command arguments to be adjusted later on for almost any NRPE command. As you begin to add more object configurations, this kind of flexibility becomes more important.

Active checks with NSClient++

Active checks for Windows clients work in much the same way as they do for Linux clients described above. First, the NSClient++ agent needs to be installed on the Windows machine. The document on the following link describes how to install the NSClient++ agent on a Windows machine:

```
http://assets.nagios.com/downloads/nagiosxi/docs/Installing_The_XI_Windows_
Agent.pdf
```

The check plugin check_nt is the default plugin used to communicate with the NSClient++ agent. The usage of the check_nt plugin is as follows:

```
 check_nt -H host -v variable -p port [-w warning] [-c critical][-l
params] [-d SHOWALL] [-t timeout] [-s password]
```

The following examples will illustrate how to carry out a new check from a command-line test to a new service definition. The command and service definitions are taken from the example configurations in the commands.cfg and windows.cfg files.

```
./check_nt -H 192.168.5.11 -v CPULOAD -s password -l 5,10,15 -p 12489
CPU Load 2% (5 min average) |    '5 min avg Load'=2%;10;15;0;100
define command{
    command_name        check_nt
```

```
    command_line           $USER1$/check_nt -H $HOSTADDRESS$ -p 12489 -v
$ARG1$ $ARG2$
}


define service{
    use                    generic-service
    host_name              winserver
    service_description    CPU Load
    check_command          check_nt!CPULOAD!-l 5,10,15
}
```

Service checks for Windows clients can range from hardware metrics, to service or process status, to Windows performance counter metrics. For more advanced features, check_nrpe can also be used with the NSClient++ agent. The NRPE listener can be enabled by following instructions in the document found at the following link:

```
http://assets.nagios.com/downloads/nagiosxi/docs/Enabling_the_NRPE_Listener_
in_NSClient.pdf
```

Passive checks for remote locations

There are some circumstances where active checks may not be suitable for a host or service that needs to be monitored. Nagios also supports the ability to push results from the client up to the Nagios server, and Nagios merely acts as the listener for check results. This is known as a passive check, since Nagios does not schedule or initiate a check for this host or service, it only processes incoming results. Passive checks are useful for the following situations:

✦ Firewall restrictions that won't allow an incoming connection to an agent

✦ Hosts that are behind a single IP address, NAT, or router

✦ Long running checks that may take a long time to complete

✦ Security related checks such as log monitoring

✦ Automation tests

NRDP (Nagios Remote Data Protocol) acts like an HTTP API for submitting check results back to Nagios. It can be used to submit Nagios commands and a batch of check results all at once. NRDP data can be sent with one of the several send_nrdp scripts that exist on exchange.nagios.org, and can be sent from almost any OS platform. At the time of writing this book, send_nrdp scripts exist in Perl, Python, and Shell. The following example illustrates configuration definitions needed for Nagios to be able to process passive checks for a host and service:

```
define host{
    host_name      My_NRDP_Host
    alias          NRDP Passive Host
    address        192.168.5.59
```

```
    use                linux-server
    check_command                  check_dummy!1!'Results are stale'
       active_checks_enabled       0
       passive_checks_enabled      1
       check_freshness             1
    freshness_checking_enabled   1
    freshness_threshold          600
}
define service{
    use                generic-service
    host_name               My_NRDP_Host
    service_description        Passive_Service
    check_command                  check_dummy!1!'Results are stale'
       active_checks_enabled       0
       passive_checks_enabled      1
       check_freshness             1
    freshness_checking_enabled   1
    freshness_threshold          10
    }
```

The previous configuration will implement the following logic for the passive checks:

✦ Do not schedule or execute this check, only listen for passive results.

✦ Check to make sure that we receive fresh results for these checks. This is known as **freshness checking**.

✦ If check results are older than 10 minutes (600 seconds), run the defined check command, check_dummy, which will alert you that your results for this host/service are stale.

See the Nagios Core manual on object definitions for a detailed explanation of each configuration directive used for hosts and services from the following link:

http://nagios.sourceforge.net/docs/nagioscore/3/en/objectdefinitions.html

Once a host and service is configured for passive checks, results can be sent via send_nrdp by using the following command:

./send_nrdp.sh -u http://myserver/nrdp -t secrettoken -H My_NRDP_Host -s Passive_Service -S 0 -o 'Everything is OK!'

send_nrdp also supports sending results directly from an XML file by using the -f flag, or a directory of files by passing the -D flag, with the directory path of the temp files. The following example illustrates an example XML file that can be specified for send_nrdp:

```
<?xml version='1.0'?>
<checkresults>
<checkresult type="host" checktype="1">
```

```
<hostname>YOUR_HOSTNAME</hostname>
<state>0</state>
<output>OK|perfdata=1.00;5;10;0</output>
</checkresult>
<checkresult type="service" checktype="1">
<hostname>YOUR_HOSTNAME</hostname>
<servicename>YOUR_SERVICENAME</servicename>
<state>0</state>
<output>OK|perfdata=1.00;5;10;0</output>
</checkresult>
</checkresults>
```

NRDP is an extremely useful tool for scaling large installations, using flexible check schedules, or monitoring remote locations.

Incident management and alerting

Setting up hosts and services is only half of effective monitoring, and is incomplete without setting up some sort of method for incident management or alerting. I once did a remote session with a user where all of the alerts from Nagios got dumped into a single inbox that had over 30,000 e-mails. During the troubleshooting of a monitoring service migration, I had asked the user if a selection of hosts had always been down on the old server, and the user didn't know, because everyone in their environment had been trained to ignore all of the alerts from Nagios and to simply filter them into an effective trash can. Without alerting, there is no monitoring taking place, so it pays to take the time to set it up properly. Nagios has an enormous amount of flexibility in how alerts and event handling can be set up, and once set up properly, can drastically increase uptime, and improve response times to any problems within an environment. Let's examine a few common scenarios and questions that users want for incident response:

1. I want to receive alerts for CPU load on a machine, but I only want alerts if the CPU load is over my threshold for at least 15 minutes.

    Behavior like this can be achieved by manipulating some of the check settings for a host or service. The following example illustrates a service check that achieves this:

    ```
    define service{
      use                     generic-service
      host_name               winserver
      service_description     CPU Load
      check_command           check_nt!CPULOAD!-l 5,10,15
      retry_interval      3
      max_check_attempts      5
    }
    ```

When Nagios detects a problem, typically, it will retry the check up to X amount of times to verify whether the problem persists before sending an alert. The max_check_attempts number specifies how many times Nagios will retry before alerting, and the retry_interval number specifies how frequently to retry the check. If Nagios detects a problem on the previously defined service, it will retry the check every 3 minutes, up to 5 times before alerting, which means that the CPU load would have to exceed a warning or critical threshold for at least 15 minutes before issuing an alert.

2. I only ever want to receive one notification for any problem that Nagios detects.

   A common scenario for many environments is to have Nagios continue to notify contacts every X number of minutes until a problem is resolved. However, if a user only wants to receive a single notification, the following settings will achieve this:

```
define service{
  use                    generic-service
  host_name              winserver
  service_description    CPU Load
  check_command          check_nt!CPULOAD!-l 5,10,15
     notification_interval   0
}
```

3. If Nagios detects that a particular service or process on a machine has stopped running, can it restart it for me?

   Besides notifications, Nagios can also run custom event handlers every time a host or service has a hard state change. The following example illustrates an HTTP check, but calls a custom script with NRPE to restart the service if a problem is detected:

```
define service{
  use             generic-service
  host_name             My_NRPE_Host
  service_description   HTTP
  check_command         check_http
  event_handler         check_nrpe_generic!restart_
httpd!'$SERVICESTATE$'
  event_handler_enabled 1
}
```

   If the previous service definition detects a hard state change for HTTP, it will submit a command to NRPE that calls a custom script to restart the httpd service. Since we don't want httpd to be restarted upon a recovery, we'll also pass it the $SERVICESTATE$ macro, which lets the restart script know if the service is okay, warning, or critical.

4. I want Nagios to alert the level one technicians if it detects a problem. However, if none of the technicians respond within three hours (or three notifications), a manager should be notified.

Nagios has the ability to define host and service **escalations**, which can even be chained together to create multiple notification levels. Escalations are triggered based on a notification count, so if X number of notifications go out to a contact, and the problem persists, Nagios notifies a new selection of contacts. Defining escalations can range from simple to very advanced, but the complete reference for escalations is documented in the Nagios Core manual, which can be found at the following link:

```
http://nagios.sourceforge.net/docs/nagioscore/3/en/escalations.html
```

5. We have servers on which we perform routine maintenance once per month, but we don't want notifications to be sent to all of the contacts every time this is done.

    Nagios allows for the use of **scheduled downtime**, which creates a time window, where Nagios will suppress any notifications or event handlers for a host, service, or group. Scheduled downtime can be either a fixed time window, or a flexible period of time. Hosts and services can even trigger downtimes to start for other hosts or services, so if a parent host goes into downtime, it will trigger a downtime start for all of the children as well. The complete documentation for scheduled downtime can be accessed with the following URL:

```
http://nagios.sourceforge.net/docs/3_0/downtime.html
```

6. Is there a way to tell Nagios to stop sending alerts even though the host or service problem still exists?

    Persistent alerts in Nagios can be suppressed for the duration of the problem by submitting an **acknowledgment**, which will suppress further alerts while the problem still persists and notifies other contacts that the issue is being worked on. Problems can be acknowledged either through the web interface or from the command line using the **external command** file nagios.cmd.

Nagios allows for the use of many administrative commands to be sent to the nagios.cmd file from the command line, such as disabling notifications, scheduling downtime, or even restarting the Nagios process. The complete reference for using external commands is located at the following URL:

```
http://old.nagios.org/developerinfo/externalcommands/
commandlist.php
```

Data visualization and reporting

Nagios is an enormous source of information for data analysis and reporting. The scope of Nagios Core is primarily intended for monitoring, alerting and event handling, and although the web interface has several built-in reports such as availability, trends, alert statistics, and the network status map, many users prefer to extend Nagios even further through the use of various add-ons in order to track historical trends in metrics, or to visualize data. Let's first examine some of the built-in reporting tools for Nagios, and then look at a few of the most popular add-ons that are used for reporting and data visualization.

Nagios reports

The Nagios Core web interface ships with several built-in tools for reporting. The Nagios Core reports mine the Nagios log archives to generate historical reports for hosts, services, and groups. The following list outlines each of the reports available with the Nagios Core CGIs, and briefly outlines what each report is used for:

✦ **Availability**: This report is essentially the standard "uptime" report for hosts and services, and can be filtered by date, host, or group.

Host State Breakdowns:

State	Type / Reason	Time	% Total Time	% Known Time
	Unscheduled	6d 22h 55m 30s	99.360%	99.360%
UP	Scheduled	0d 0h 0m 0s	0.000%	0.000%
	Total	6d 22h 55m 30s	99.360%	99.360%
	Unscheduled	0d 1h 4m 30s	0.640%	0.640%
DOWN	Scheduled	0d 0h 0m 0s	0.000%	0.000%
	Total	0d 1h 4m 30s	0.640%	0.640%
	Unscheduled	0d 0h 0m 0s	0.000%	0.000%
UNREACHABLE	Scheduled	0d 0h 0m 0s	0.000%	0.000%
	Total	0d 0h 0m 0s	0.000%	0.000%
	Nagios Not Running	0d 0h 0m 0s	0.000%	
Undetermined	Insufficient Data	0d 0h 0m 0s	0.000%	
	Total	0d 0h 0m 0s	0.000%	
All	Total	7d 0h 0m 0s	100.000%	100.000%

State Breakdowns For Host Services:

Service	% Time OK	% Time Warning	% Time Unknown	% Time Critical	% Time Undetermined
Bugtest notifications enabled	100.000% (100.000%)	0.000% (0.000%)	0.000% (0.000%)	0.000% (0.000%)	0.000%
CPU Usage	92.159% (92.159%)	0.000% (0.000%)	7.196% (7.196%)	0.645% (0.645%)	0.000%
Drive C: Disk Usage	92.161% (92.161%)	0.000% (0.000%)	7.196% (7.196%)	0.643% (0.643%)	0.000%
Drive D: Disk Usage	92.111% (99.253%)	0.000% (0.000%)	0.000% (0.000%)	0.693% (0.747%)	7.196%
Memory Usage	92.158% (99.303%)	0.000% (0.000%)	0.000% (0.000%)	0.646% (0.697%)	7.196%
Ping	99.355% (99.355%)	0.000% (0.000%)	0.000% (0.000%)	0.645% (0.645%)	0.000%
Uptime	92.161% (99.307%)	0.000% (0.000%)	0.000% (0.000%)	0.643% (0.693%)	7.196%
Average	94.301% (97.363%)	0.000% (0.000%)	2.056% (2.056%)	0.559% (0.581%)	3.084%

✦ **Trends**: This report visually represents the state history and uptime of a single host or service.

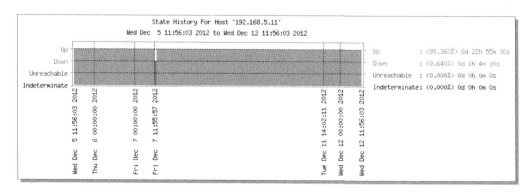

✦ **Alerts**: Typically tracking alerts is a straight-forward way to identify the most problematic hosts and services in the network infrastructure. The alert reports can be represented as a list with the History report, a table using the Summary report, and as a graph using the Histogram report.

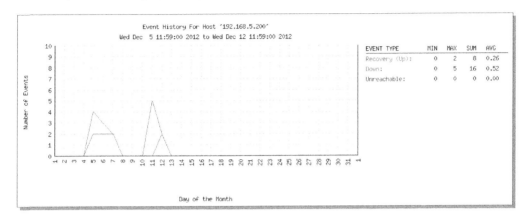

✦ **Map**: This is more of a visualization tool than a report, but can be very useful for visualizing the network health in a topology view, as shown in the following screenshot:

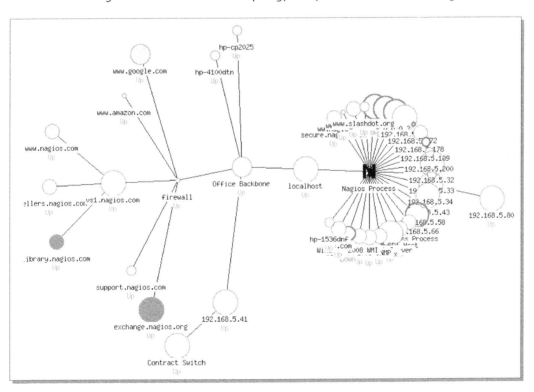

Performance graphing

Most of the check plugins that you'll find with Nagios return **performance data**, which is some form of performance metric that can be passed to an external graphing tool. Most often this data is passed to an **RRD** (**Round Robin Database**) file, which is a binary storage file that never grows in size. Using an add-on project such as PNP4Nagios or Nagiosgraph allows you to store performance metrics in RRD files and view them on a graph for as far back as four years.

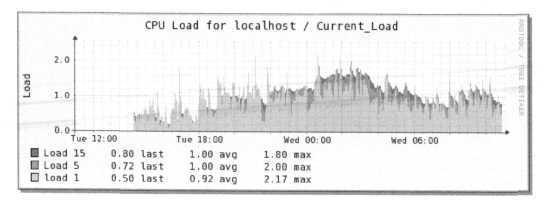

More information and documentation for these projects can be found on the following project home pages:

+ PNP4Nagios: http://www.pnp4nagios.org/

+ Nagiosgraph: http://sourceforge.net/projects/nagiosgraph/

NagVis

NagVis is a visualization add-on for Nagios that allows for custom maps and diagrams to be built, which contain live status information from Nagios. This tool is enormously flexible to create custom visualizations.

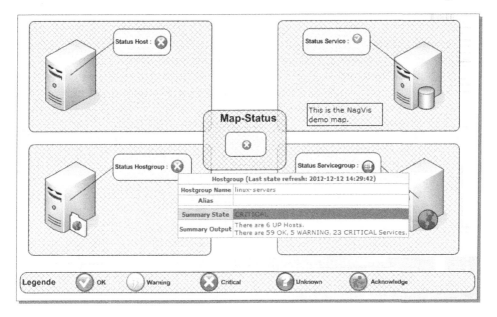

NagVis project home can be found at http://www.nagvis.org/.

Nagios BPI

Nagios Business Process Intelligence (**Nagios BPI**) is a way to visualize and monitor business processes that are made up of many hosts, services, and even other BPI groups. Nagios BPI is used by many users to monitor the real state of the network and allows for rules and thresholds to be defined for business processes, so that their states can be effectively monitored.

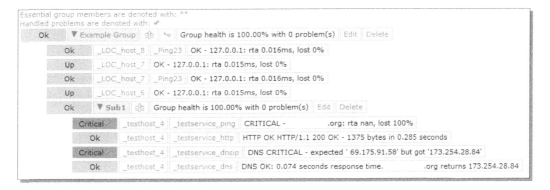

The Nagios BPI add-on is available at exchange.nagios.org.

Ndoutils

Ndoutils provides a database backend for all monitoring data that is processed by the Nagios Core monitoring engine. Many users have a need to use their own custom reporting tools, and prefer a database backend for historical information as opposed to mining log archives to create custom reports. Ndoutils supports multiple Nagios servers storing data on a local or remote database server.

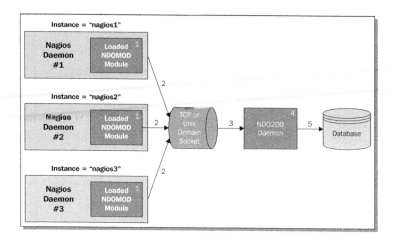

The Ndoutils add-on is available on `exchange.nagios.org`.

Nagios basic troubleshooting

Nagios creates unique challenges for troubleshooting and debugging, not only because so much of what it does is tied to the environment that it's installed on, but also because it depends largely on what's being monitored. Knowing where to look for clues and when to ask for help are essential steps to getting started with Nagios. The following list identifies some key places to look for clues in troubleshooting problems with Nagios:

- ✦ `/usr/local/nagios/var/nagios.log`: This is the primary log file for Nagios, which records not only all monitoring engine events and alerts, but also configuration errors and runtime errors.

- ✦ `/var/log/messages`: This is the generic syslog for Linux systems, although this file may differ depending on the Linux distribution used. This file logs key system events and errors, and can be especially useful in troubleshooting issues with NRPE or SNMP.

- ✦ `iptables -l`: This command lists open ports on the current machine. One of the biggest culprits for a problem with monitoring is a firewall rule blocking the traffic.

- ✦ **Nagios support**: The Nagios community is enormous, and the chances are that someone has gone through similar issues. The following URL is the Nagios support home page, and is the best place to start for getting more documentation and forum support:

  `http://support.nagios.com`

People and places you should get to know

Nagios is a project with an enormous ecosystem of plugins, add-ons, and extensions, and the community that surrounds it is enormous. With such a broad community, knowing where to start looking for resources is extremely important. If you need help with Nagios, the following section provides the whereabouts of some people and places that will prove invaluable.

Official sites

+ Community homepage: www.nagios.org

+ Commercial homepage: www.nagios.com

+ Manual and documentation: nagios.sourceforge.net/docs/3_0/

+ Support forum: support.nagios.com/forum

+ Wiki: support.nagios.com/wiki/

+ Blog: labs.nagios.com

+ Source code: sourceforge.net/projects/nagios/

+ Nagios projects: exchange.nagios.org

Articles and tutorials

+ Begin Linux: *Central Monitoring with Nagios and NSCA*

    http://beginlinux.com/blog/2010/03/nagios-central-monitoring/

+ Roshamboot tech blog: *Monitoring ESX/vCenter like a less crazy person*

    http://roshamboot.org/main/?p=169

+ Roshamboot tech blog: *Effective User and Contact Management with Nagios*

    http://roshamboot.org/main/?p=193

Communities

+ Official forums: http://support.nagios.com/forum

+ Official mailing list: nagios-users@lists.sourceforge.net

+ Official IRC channel: #nagios on Freenode

+ User FAQ: http://support.nagios.com/wiki/

Blogs

✦ Nagios entperises tech blog for new developments, documentation, and tutorials: `labs.nagios.com`

✦ Begin Linux: *Linux Training for the Desktop and Server* at `www.beginlinux.com`

✦ Rock Beats Server. Active Nagios community member John Murphy's tutorials and tech tips at `roshamboot.org`

Twitter

✦ Follow Ethan Galstad, father of Nagios on Twitter at `http://twitter.com/#!/fatherofnagios`

✦ Follow Nagios Inc at `http://twitter.com/#!/nagiosinc`

✦ Follow Michael Guthrie, author of *Instant Nagios Starter, Packt Publishing* at `http://twitter.com/#!/mguthrie88`

✦ Follow Begin Linux, author of Linux and Nagios tutorials and training at `http://twitter.com/#!/beginlinux`

✦ For more open source information, follow Packt Publishing at `http://twitter.com/#!/packtopensource`

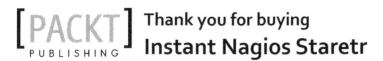

Thank you for buying
Instant Nagios Staretr

About Packt Publishing

Packt, pronounced 'packed', published its first book "*Mastering phpMyAdmin for Effective MySQL Management*" in April 2004 and subsequently continued to specialize in publishing highly focused books on specific technologies and solutions.

Our books and publications share the experiences of your fellow IT professionals in adapting and customizing today's systems, applications, and frameworks. Our solution based books give you the knowledge and power to customize the software and technologies you're using to get the job done. Packt books are more specific and less general than the IT books you have seen in the past. Our unique business model allows us to bring you more focused information, giving you more of what you need to know, and less of what you don't.

Packt is a modern, yet unique publishing company, which focuses on producing quality, cutting-edge books for communities of developers, administrators, and newbies alike. For more information, please visit our website: www.packtpub.com.

Writing for Packt

We welcome all inquiries from people who are interested in authoring. Book proposals should be sent to author@packtpub.com. If your book idea is still at an early stage and you would like to discuss it first before writing a formal book proposal, contact us; one of our commissioning editors will get in touch with you.

We're not just looking for published authors; if you have strong technical skills but no writing experience, our experienced editors can help you develop a writing career, or simply get some additional reward for your expertise.

Learning Nagios 3.0

ISBN: 978-1-84719-518-0   Paperback: 316 pages

A detailed tutorial to setting up, configuring, and managing this easy and effective system monitoring software

1. Secure and monitor your network system with open-source Nagios version 3

2. Set up, configure, and manage the latest version of Nagios

3. In-depth coverage for both beginners and advanced users

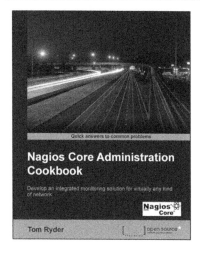

Nagios Core Administration Cookbook

ISBN: 978-1-84951-556-6   Paperback: 360 pages

Develop an integrated monitoring solution for virtually any kind of network

1. Monitor almost anything in a network

2. Control notifications in your network by configuring Nagios Core

3. Get a handle on best practices and time-saving configuration methods for a leaner configuration

4. Use the web interface to control notification behaviour on the fly and for scheduled outages, without restarts

5. Pull Nagios Core's data into a database to write clever custom reports of your own devising

Please check **www.PacktPub.com** for information on our titles

Zenoss Core 3.x Network and System Monitoring

ISBN: 978-1-84951-158-2   Paperback: 312 pages

A step-by-step guid to configuring, using, and adapting this free Open Source network monitoring system

1. Designed to quickly acquaint you with the core feature so you can customize Zenoss Core to your needs

2. Discover, manage, and monitor IT resources

3. Build custom event-processing and alerting rules

4. Write custom device reports to extract, display, and analyze monitoring data

Zenoss Core Network and System Monitoring

ISBN: 978-1-84719-428-2   Paperback: 280 pages

A step-by-step guid to configuring, using, and adapting the free Open Source network monitoring system

1. Discover, manage, and monitor IT resources

2. Build custom event processing and alerting rules

3. Configure Zenoss Core via an easy to use web interface

4. Drag and drop dashboard portlets with Google Maps integration

Please check **www.PacktPub.com** for information on our titles

61753146R00027